My Tail Is Long and Striped

by Joyce Markovics

Consultants:
Christopher Kuhar, PhD
Executive Director
Cleveland Metroparks Zoo
Cleveland, Ohio

Kimberly Brenneman, PhD
National Institute for Early Education Research
Rutgers University
New Brunswick, New Jersey

BEARPORT
PUBLISHING

New York, New York

Credits

Cover, © Hemera/Thinkstock; 4–5, © iStockphoto/Thinkstock; 6–7, © LVV/Shutterstock; 8–9, © David Ryznar/Shutterstock; 10–11, © Skifenok/Dreamstime.com; 12–13, © David & Micha Sheldon; 14–15, © Hal Brindley/Shutterstock; 16–17, © Hemera/Thinkstock; 18–19, © iStockphoto/Thinkstock; 20–21, © iStockphoto/Thinkstock; 22, © iStockphoto/Thinkstock; 23, © NREY/Shutterstock; 24T, © NREY/Shutterstock; 24B, © iStockphoto/Thinkstock.

Publisher: Kenn Goin
Senior Editor: Joyce Tavolacci
Creative Director: Spencer Brinker
Design: Debrah Kaiser
Photo Researcher: Michael Win

Library of Congress Cataloging-in-Publication Data

Markovics, Joyce L.
 My tail is long and striped / by Joyce Markovics ; consultant: Christopher Kuhar, PhD, Executive Director, Cleveland Metroparks Zoo, Cleveland, Ohio.
     pages cm. — (Zoo clues)
 Includes bibliographical references and index.
 ISBN-13: 978-1-62724-107-6 (library binding)
 ISBN-10: 1-62724-107-8 (library binding)
 1. Ring-tailed lemur—Juvenile literature. I. Title.
 QL737.P95M36 2014
 599.8'3—dc23
                                        2013035386

For more information, write to Bearport Publishing Company, Inc., 45 West 21st Street, Suite 3B, New York, New York 10010. Printed in the United States of America.

10 9 8 7 6 5 4 3 2 1

Contents

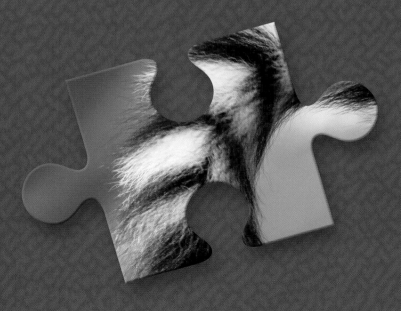

What Am I?

Look at my eyes.

They are large
and yellow.

My ears are
white and fuzzy.

I have a round, black nose.

9

My fur is thick.

10

It is gray
and white.

11

12

I have five fingers on each hand.

13

My teeth are
sharp and white.

15

I have a long,
striped tail.

16

The stripes are black and white.

What am I?

18

Let's find out!

19

I am a ring-tailed lemur!

21

Animal Facts

Ring-tailed lemurs are mammals. Like almost all mammals, they give birth to live young. The babies drink milk from their mothers. Mammals also have hair or fur on their skin.

More Ring-tailed Lemur Facts

Food:	Fruit, flowers, leaves, tree bark, and tree sap
Size:	40 inches (102 cm) long, including the tail
Weight:	Up to 7.5 pounds (3.4 kg)
Life Span:	Up to 18 years in the wild
Cool Fact:	Ring-tailed lemurs have special teeth that they use to comb their fur.

Adult Lemur Size

Where Do I Live?

Ring-tailed lemurs live on the African island of Madagascar. They live in forests, where they jump from tree to tree.

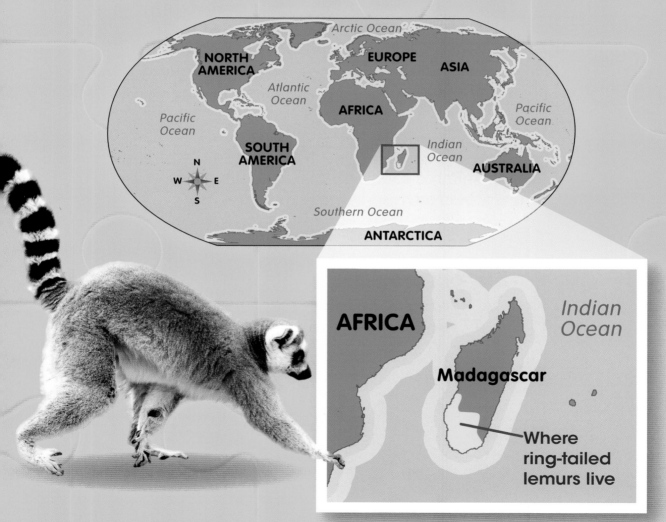

Where ring-tailed lemurs live

Index

Read More

Ganeri, Anita. *Lemur (A Day in the Life: Rain Forest Animals).* Chicago: Heinemann (2011).

Riley, Joelle. *Ring-Tailed Lemurs (Early Bird Nature Books).* Minneapolis, MN: Lerner (2009).

Learn More Online

To learn more about ring-tailed lemurs, visit **www.bearportpublishing.com/ZooClues**

About the Author

Joyce Markovics lives along the Hudson River in Tarrytown, New York. She enjoys spending time with furry, finned, and feathered creatures.